Interest and Its Role in Economy and Life
(English)

الربا وأثره على الحياة والاقتصاد

(إنجليزي)

Jamaal al-Din Zarabozo

جمال الدين زارابوزو

Interest and Its Role in Economy and Life (1 of 8):
An Introduction
(English)

الربا وأثره على الحياة والاقتصاد : ١- مقدمة و مدخل

(إنجليزي)

Jamaal al-Din Zarabozo

جمال الدين زارابوزو

Introduction

Interest is defined in the *Oxford English Dictionary* as, "Money paid for the use of money lent (the principal), or for forbearance of a debt, according to a fixed ratio."[1]

Actually, individuals and the world as a whole probably know too well the burden of interest, such that no one truly needs the above definition. Interest is something that is known to anyone living in a capitalist country. It has become so completely institutionalized and accepted in modern economies that it is almost impossible to conceive that there are some who completely oppose it and refuse any transactions that involve interest. But there are devout Muslims who refuse to deal in interest.

The actual reason why such Muslims do not deal with interest is that interest has been forbidden by the Islamic religion, as shall be detailed shortly. At the same time, though, Muslims believe that God's guidance is based on His knowledge, wisdom and justice. In other words, God does not forbid something from humans for no reason whatsoever. Hence, there are definitely sound reasons—some of which we may be able to clearly recognize—why God has forbidden this practice.

In today's world, Muslims are constantly being bombarded with arguments in support of dealing with interest. Many Muslims have succumbed to such pressure and supposedly rational arguments, leading them to accept the concept of interest.

Therefore, this short article is intended to discuss the Islamic stance on interest as based on the basic texts of the faith as well as enter into a rational discussion of interest to determine if the arguments given in favor of interest are truly valid.

God's Guidance for Mankind

Islam teaches that God has mercifully given guidance to humankind for all aspects of life. This guidance covers not just acts of worship but everything from economics and business ethics to marital relations, international relations, ethics of warfare and so forth. It is one of the distinguishing

---

[1] *Oxford English Dictionary Software* (Oxford, England: Oxford University Press, 2002), entry, "interest."

traits of Muslims today that they still believe in such guidance from God while so many among humankind have discarded or preempted their religious teachings when it comes to "secular" issues.

There are a number of reasons why many Muslims have not followed the same path that, for example, numerous secular Jews and Christians have followed. One of the most important reasons is that the Muslim can be confident that the revelation which forms the basis of the Islamic religion has not been tampered with or distorted since the time of its revelation. In other words, there has been no human interference or distortion in the revelation. Hence, there is no need for humans to come along now and fix the mistakes of earlier humans, as secular Jews or Christians would argue. Indeed, the only result for Muslims would be humans, by their interference, damaging the revelation that has come from God.

Second, many Muslims believe that they have not been shown any strong or convincing evidence that somehow their religion is out of touch with reality or impractical in modern times. In Islam, for example, there has never been a conflict between religion and science, leading to a breakdown of trust in the church and a virtual revolt against the authority of religion as experienced in the West.[1] Many people, even some Muslims, have

---

[1] A classic work on the history of the Christian/European experience concerning the conflict between religion and science is John William Draper, *History of the Conflict between Religion and Science* (Order of Thelemic Knights, 2005). Note that his title should actually be corrected, since it is the history of the conflict between science and Christianity in Europe. In his work, *A History of the Intellectual Development of Europe* (Honolulu, Hawaii: University Press of the Pacific, 2002), the same John William Draper divides the history of Europe into the age of faith followed by the age of reason, highlighting once again the conflict that exists in Christianity in particular (but also in Judaism) but "reason" and "science" vis-à-vis "faith." Again, Islam has never experienced such a crisis. In fact, Islam's consistency with modern science is something that has actually drawn many converts into Islam. For example, a non-Muslim professor, Prof. Tejatat Tejasen of Chiang Mai University in Thailand, studied the relationship between Islam and modern science and finally stated the following:

"During the last three years, I became interested in the Quran… From my study… I believe that everything that has been recorded in the Quran fourteen hundred years ago must be the truth, that can be proved by scientific means. Since the Prophet Muhammad could neither read nor write, Muhammad must be a messenger who relayed this truth, which was revealed to him as an enlightenment by the one who is eligible [as the] creator… Therefore, I think this is the time to say… [at this point, Prof. Tejasen makes a declaration of Islamic faith]." [Quoted from I. A. Ibrahim, *A Brief Illustrated Guide to Understanding Islam* (Houston: Darussalam, 1997), p. 31.

called for many changes within Islam but, in reality, the arguments that they have presented have been faulty and flimsy, to say the least. The case of interest, this article's topic, can be taken as an excellent example of this nature.

This work, in its entirety, is available at www.islam-guide.com. Ibrahim reviews and summarizes the conclusions of many contemporary scientists.]

Interest and Its Role in Economy and Life (2 of 8):
The Islamic Stance
(English)

الربا وأثره على الحياة والاقتصاد : ٢- موقف الإسلام من الربا

(إنجليزي)

Jamaal al-Din Zarabozo

جمال الدين زارابوزو

The Islamic Texts on Interest

When one reads the Islamic texts concerning interest, one is immediately taken by how stringent the warnings are against any involvement in interest. Islam prohibits a number of immoral acts such as fornication, adultery, homosexuality, consuming alcohol and murder. But the variety of discussion and extent of warnings for these other acts is not of the same level of those related to taking interest. This has led Sayyid Qutb to write, "No other issue has been condemned and denounced so strongly in the Quran as has usury."[1]

The Quran, for example, contains the following verses concerning interest[2]:

"O you who have believed, do not consume interest, doubled and multiplied, but fear God that you may be successful. And fear the Fire, which has been prepared for the disbelievers." **(Quran 3:130-131)**

This rather strong warning towards the believers warns of a fatal consequence: being thrown into the Hell-fire that has been prepared for the disbelievers.

God also says:

"Those who consume interest cannot stand [on the Day of Resurrection] except as one stands who is being beaten by Satan into insanity. That is because they say, 'Trade is [just] like interest.' But God has permitted

---

[1] Sayyid Qutb, *In the Shade of the Quran* (Markfield, Leicester, England: The Islamic Foundation, 1999), vol. 1, p. 355

[2] The Arabic word used in these verses of the Quran is *ribaa*. *Ribaa* can be defined as, "an excess and an addition; an addition over and above the principal sum [that is lent or expended]." Cf., E. W. Lane, *Arabic-English Lexicon* (Cambridge, England: The Islamic Texts Society, 1984), vol. 1, 1023. Unfortunately, some translators of the Quran (including Abdullah Yusuf Ali, Khan and al-Hilali, and Pickthall) chose to translate the word *ribaa* as "usury." This has led to some confusion, even among Western Muslims. *The Oxford English Dictionary* defines usury as, "The fact or practice of lending money at interest; esp. in later use, the practice of charging, taking, or contracting to receive, excessive or illegal rates of interest for money on loan." In other words, at one time, the word "usury" was equivalent to the act of lending money on interest, back when this was still a despised act. After interest became completely legalized, the word usury began to mean "lending at excessive or illegal rates." The Arabic term *ribaa*, in contemporary terms, must be translated as "interest" since it includes any and all payments made in addition to or above the principal.

trade and has forbidden interest. So whoever has received an admonition from his Lord and desists may have what is past, and his affair rests with God. But whoever returns [to dealing in interest or usury]—those are the companions of the Fire; they will abide eternally therein. God destroys interest and gives increase for charities. And God does not like every sinning disbeliever." (Quran 2:275-276)

These verses have many interesting points to them. Commenting on the first portion of the verse, Maudoodi has written,

Just as an insane person, unconstrained by ordinary reason, resorts to all kinds of immoderate acts, so does one who takes interest. He pursues his craze for money as if he were insane. He is heedless of the fact that interest cuts the very roots of human love, brotherhood and fellow-feeling, and undermines the welfare and happiness of human society, and that his enrichment is at the expense of the well-being of many other human beings. This is the state of his "insanity" in this world: since a man will rise in the Hereafter in the same state in which he dies in the present world, he will be resurrected as a lunatic.[1]

Secondly, the verses make it quite clear that there is a difference between legitimate business transactions and interest. The difference between them is so glaring that the verse does not bother to explain them, which is one of the stylistic aspects of the Quran. Thirdly, these verses clearly state that God "destroys interest and gives increase for charities." This is one of God's "laws" which humankind cannot necessarily discover on its own. The ultimate and full negative effects of interest on the individual, community and world as a whole in both this life and the Hereafter are known only to God. However, a glimpse of some of those negative effects, testifying to the truth of this verse, shall be given later in this paper. In fact, perhaps highlighting the meaning of this verse, the Prophet (peace and blessings of God be upon him) also said, "Interest— even it is a large amount— in the end will result in a small amount."[2] Undoubtedly, in the Hereafter

---

[1] Sayyid Abu Ala Mawdudi, *Towards Understanding the Quran* (Leicester, United Kingdom: The Islamic Foundation, 1988), vol. 1, p. 213.

[2] Recorded by al-Hakim. See al-Albani, *Sahih al-Jami al-Sagheer*, vol. 1, p. 664, hadith no. 3543. Interest is all about amassing more money, even without putting the money at risk. This, in the long-run, however, does not necessarily produce happiness: "General Social Survey (GSS) study reported in Business Week (October 16, 2000) concluded that money was not buying happiness and the new life style and its aftershocks are causing the rise of unhappiness. According to that study, although there was a per capita increase in income

when the individual meets God, all that he amassed via such illegal means will be a source of his own destruction.

Shortly after the above verses, God further says,

"O you who have believed, fear God and give up what remains [due to you] of interest, if you should be believers. And if you do not, then be informed of a war [against you] from God and His Messenger. But if you repent, you may have your principal—[thus] you do no wrong [to others], nor are you wronged." (Quran 2:278-279)

Who in his right mind would expose himself to a declaration of war from God and His Messenger? Undoubtedly, a stronger threat one will rarely find. At the end of the verse, God makes it very clear why interest is forbidden: it is wrongdoing. The Arabic word for such is *dhulm*, meaning a person has done wrong to, harmed or oppressed another person or his own soul. This verse demonstrates that interest is not forbidden simply due to some ruling of God without any rationale behind that ruling. Interest is definitely harmful and therefore it has been forbidden.

In addition to the verses of the Quran, the Prophet Muhammad (peace and blessings of God be upon him) also made many statements concerning interest. For example, the following statement clearly demonstrates the gravity of this action:

"Avoid the seven destructive sins: associating partners with God, sorcery, killing a soul which God has forbidden— except through due course of the law, devouring interest, devouring the wealth of orphans, fleeing when the armies meet, and slandering chaste, believing, innocent women." (*al-Bukhari and Muslim*)

---

between 1970 and 1998, Americans, to the contrary, grew less happy. The new social tendencies overshadowed any material gains. The study found that although extra income brings extra happiness, such impact was surprisingly poor. It also found that factors, such as gender and material status, weigh more heavily. Another find was that women are growing more unhappy than men. The increase in divorce and separation between spouses is having a negative impact on the family structure and the psychology of its members. Business Week concluded: 'At the very least, it suggests that those who think income gains alone guarantee greater happiness are deluding themselves. And it implies that some apparent aspects of the New Economy, such as more bouts of unemployment and greater income inequality, carry significant psychological costs.'" **Abdulhay Y. Zalloum,** *Painting Islam as the New Enemy: Globalization & Capitalism in Crisis* (Technology One Group S.A. 2002), p. 357.

In fact, another statement of the Prophet (peace and blessings of Allah be upon him) should be sufficient to keep any God-fearing individual completely away from interest. The Prophet (peace and blessings of Allah be upon him) said:

"One coin of interest that is knowingly consumed by a person is worse in God's sight than thirty-six acts of illegal sexual intercourse." (*al-Tabarani and al-Hakim*)

The Companion Jaabir narrated that the Messenger of God (peace and blessings of God be upon him) cursed the one who takes interest, the one who pays interest, the witnesses to it [that is, the interest contracts] and the recorder of it. Then he said, "They are all the same." (*Muslim*)

This is a basic principle in Islam. If something is forbidden and wrong, a Muslim should not participate in it or support it in any fashion. Thus, since interest is forbidden, it is also forbidden to be a witness to such contracts, to record them and so on. The Prophet's words also explain that there is no difference between the one who pays interest and the one who receives it. This is because they are both involved in a despicable practice and, hence, they are equally culpable.

The Prophet Muhammad (peace and blessings of Allah be upon him) also said,

"If illicit sexual relations and interest openly appear in a town, they have opened themselves to the punishment of God." (*al-Tabarani and al-Hakim*)

This statement is a reference to one of God's "societal laws." The punishment of God may come in different forms in this world or the next.

Interest and Its Role in Economy and Life (3 of 8):

Religion and Early Thinkers

(English)

الربا وأثره على الحياة والاقتصاد : ٣- موقف الدين و المفكرين الأوائل

(إنجليزي)

Jamaal al-Din Zarabozo

جمال الدين زارابوزو

Islam, of course, is not the only religion that has banned interest and considered it a despicable practice. The prohibition of interest—at least to some extent—is a well-known law in both the Old and the New Testaments of the Bible. In numerous places in the Old Testament, reference has been made to "usury" or "interest." (Again, usury and interest used to be equivalent but only over time did usury begin to mean an exorbitant or illegal amount of interest. Thus, as shall be noted below, the *American Standard Version* of the Bible repeatedly changed the *King James Version* from usury to interest.)

Deuteronomy 23:19-20 reads:

"Thou shalt not lend upon usury to thy brother; usury of money, usury of victuals, usury of any thing that is lent upon usury: Unto a stranger thou mayest lend upon usury; but unto thy brother thou shalt not lend upon usury: that the LORD thy God may bless thee in all that thou settest thine hand to in the land whither thou goest to possess it" (*King James Version*).[1]

Similarly, Exodus 22:25 states:

"If thou lend money to any of my people that is poor by thee, thou shalt not be to him as an usurer, neither shalt thou lay upon him usury" (*King James Version*).[2]

In Leviticus 25:37 one reads:

"Thou shalt not give him thy money upon usury, nor lend him thy victuals for increase" (*King James Version*).[3]

---

[1] The *American Standard Version* reads, "Thou shalt not lend upon interest to thy brother; interest of money, interest of victuals, interest of anything that is lent upon interest: unto a foreigner thou mayest lend upon interest; but unto thy brother thou shalt not lend upon interest, that Jehovah thy God may bless thee in all that thou puttest thy hand unto, in the land whither thou goest in to possess it." **Note that all quotes from Bibles, Biblical commentaries or Biblical dictionaries are, unless otherwise noted, from** *The Bible Collection CD* (ValueSoft, 2007).

[2] "If thou lend money to any of my people with thee that is poor, thou shalt not be to him as a creditor; neither shall ye lay upon him interest" (*American Standard Version*).

[3] "Thou shalt not give him thy money upon interest, nor give him thy victuals for increase" (*American Standard Version*).

In Jeremiah 15:10, the Prophet complains that he is being cursed although he has never done anything such as take interest, meaning that such curses would be appropriate for him if he were someone who took interest. Perhaps one of the harshest verses in the Old Testament concerning interest is Ezekiel 18:13:

"Hath given forth upon interest, and hath taken increase: shall he then live? he shall not live: he hath done all these abominations; he shall surely die; his blood shall be upon him."

There are yet other verses of the Old Testament that indicate the prohibition of interest but what has been presented above should suffice.[1] *Easton's Bible Dictionary* has summarized the Mosaic Law concerning interest in the following passage:

The Mosaic law required that when an Israelite needed to borrow, what he asked was to be freely lent to him, and no interest was to be charged, although interest might be taken of a foreigner (Exodus 22:25; Deuteronomy 23:19,20; Leviticus 25:35-38). At the end of seven years all debts were remitted. Of a foreigner the loan might, however, be exacted. At a later period of the Hebrew commonwealth, when commerce increased, the practice of exacting usury or interest on loans, and of suretiship in the commercial sense, grew up. Yet the exaction of it from a Hebrew was regarded as discreditable (Psalms 15:5; Proverbs 6:1,4; 11:15; 17:18; 20:16; 27:13; Jeremiah 15:10).

Unfortunately, as is often the case on practical issues, the New Testament is somewhat vague on the issue of interest. According to *The Encyclopedia of Religion and Ethics*, "there are no direct precepts [concerning interest] to guide the Christian conscience."[2] However, in the teachings attributed to Jesus in the New Testament, there are some passages that seem to be clearly against the practice of interest. In one passage, Jesus is reported to have said:

---

[1] Cf., Psalms 15:1-5; Ezekiel 18:5-9 and Proverbs 28:8. The Old Testament also verifies that although the Jews were prohibited from taking interest, they were often guilty of falling into that act. See Nehemiah 5:6-7 and Ezekiel 22:12.

[2] Quoted from Abdelmoneim El-Gousi, "Riba, Islamic Law and Interest" (Ph.D. Dissertation, Temple University, 1982), p. 113.

"But love ye your enemies, and do good, and lend, hoping for nothing again; and your reward shall be great, and ye shall be the children of the Highest: for he is kind unto the unthankful and to the evil" (**Luke 6:35**).

In this passage, Christians are actually told to lend out money without hoping to receive the principal again. This may be considered one of the "hard sayings" and, as is well-known, Christian scholars differ as to how such passages are to be interpreted and implemented.[1]

In Matthew 25:14-28, there is a lengthy parable wherein God gives different amounts of coins (called "talents") to various servants. Some of them invest the money and bring back more to God than what God gave them. However, the person to whom God only gave one such coin is described in verse 18:

"But he that had received one went and digged in the earth, and hid his lord's money."

When God calls back His servants and asks about what they did with the money, the one who received only one talent stated to God:

"Then he which had received the one talent came and said, Lord, I knew thee that thou art an hard man, reaping where thou hast not sown, and gathering where thou hast not strowed: And I was afraid, and went and hid thy talent in the earth: lo, there thou hast that is thine" (*Matthew* 25:24-25).

The Lord then sternly replies to him:

"His lord answered and said unto him, Thou wicked and slothful servant, thou knewest that I reap where I sowed not, and gather where I have not strowed: Thou oughtest therefore to have put my money to the exchangers, and then at my coming I should have received mine own with usury. Take therefore the talent from him, and give it unto him which hath ten talents" (*Matthew* 25:26-28).

Commenting on this passage, the *Geneva Study Bible* states,

---

[1] Do such sayings represent a perfectionist code, an impossible ideal, an "interim ethic," or something else? Christian scholars have not been able to agree on the answer to this question. Cf., Lisa Sowle Cahill, *Love Your Enemies: Discipleship, Pacifism, and Just War Theory* (Minneapolis, MN: Fortress Press, 1994), p. 27.

Bankers who have their shops or tables set up abroad, where they lend money at interest. Usury or loaning money at interest is strictly forbidden by the Bible, (Exodus 22:25-27; Deuteronomy 23:19, 20). Even a rate as low as one per cent interest was disallowed, (Nehemiah 5:11). This servant had already told two lies. First he said the master was an austere or harsh man. This is a lie for the Lord is merciful and gracious. Next he called his master a thief because he reaped where he did not sow. Finally the master said to him sarcastically why did you not add insult to injury and loan the money out at interest so you could call your master a "usurer" too! If the servant had done this, his master would have been responsible for his servant's actions and guilty of usury.

Based on the Old and New Testaments, the early Church Councils disallowed interest. Eventually all Christians were prohibited from indulging in interest, not simply the clergy. Christian fathers, such as St. Thomas Aquinas[1], dealt with the issue of interest in some detail. "In the Decree of Gratian, as subsequently at the Third Lateran Council (1179), a canon ordained that 'manifest usurers shall not be admitted to communion, nor, if they die in their sin, receive Christian burial.'"[2] The Fourth Lateran Council of 1215 condemned the practice but allowed it for the Jews. Catholics remained firmly against interest until the 19th Century. Martin Luther of the 16th Century, the Protestant leader, also condemned usury but, it is claimed, he allowed on it on a plea of human weakness.[3] Calvin, more than anyone else, was the beginning of a softer view concerning interest among Christian leaders. Slowly civil legislation freed itself from Canon Law and interest began to be institutionalized over time.

It was not only those of the Judeo-Christian thinking that condemned interest. In fact, the Greek philosophers also took a very negative view of interest. Aristotle and other leading Greek scholars condemned interest. The famed Austrian economist, Eugen von Böhm von Bawerk (also known as Boehm-Bawerk), wrote in his important work, *Capital and Interest*,

---

[1] A review of Aquinas' thoughts on interest may be found in Rodney Wilson, *Economics, Ethics and Religion: Jewish, Christian and Muslim Economic Thought* (Washington Square, New York: New York University Press, 1997), pp. 82-85. In reality, though, like much of the Christian thought on just war, Aquinas was heavily influenced by pre-Christian Greek and Roman thought.
[2] El-Gousi, p. 114.
[3] Cf., Anwar Iqbal Qureshi, *Islam and the Theory of Interest* (Lahore, Pakistan: Sh. Muhammad Ashraf Publications, 1974), p. 8.

The hostile expressions of the ancient world, not few in number, consist, in part, of a number of legislative acts forbidding the taking of interest and in part accidental utterance of philosophers such as Plato, Aristotle, the two Catos, Cicero, Seneca and Pantus etc. Greek philosophers regarded money as nothing but a medium of exchange and, therefore, they denied the productivity of money loans. A piece of money cannot beget another piece was the doctrine of Aristotle. The obvious conclusion was that interest is unjust.[1]

Initially, the Roman Empire as well prohibited the charging of interest. With the rise of trading classes, this was lessened a bit but there were still severe restrictions on interest lending as well as laws to protect debtors.

Shakespeare's character Shylock in *The Merchant of Venice* (written just prior to the year 1600) demonstrates just how despised moneylenders who dealt in interest were. The obvious qu

estion arises as to how interest went from being a despised and forbidden act to a socially acceptable and institutionalized practice in the West.

---

[1] Boehm Bawerk, *Capital and Interest* (1959), Vol. I, pp. 10-11, Quoted from Afzal-ur-Rahman, *Economic Doctrines of Islam* (Lahore, Pakistan: Islamic Publications Limited, 1976), vol. III, p. 11. Also see Qureshi, p. 6; El-Gousi, p. 114.

Interest and Its Role in Economy and Life (4 of 8): Prohibition to Justification

(English)

الربا وأثره على الحياة والاقتصاد : ٤- من التحريم إلى التبرير

(إنجليزي)

Jamaal al-Din Zarabozo

جمال الدين زارابوزو

Over time, it was considered that the prohibition of interest was nothing more than a religious dogma that needed to be done away with. Religion could no longer be allowed to run economics. This was certainly the sentiment expressed by famed economist historian Richard Tawney when he stated,

"The whole scheme of medieval thought attempted to treat economic affairs as a part of hierarchy of values embracing all interest and activities of which the apex was religion."[1] At the same time, though, it seems that the change in attitude that took place was not based on purely economic reasons. Lawrence Dennis stated,

Aristotle, the Roman Catholic Canonists, the Jewish Torah. . . all forbade loans at interest, or denounced interest as usury. Lending at interest took its rise in the medieval centuries largely as a matter of accommodating princes who needed and could not raise enough money for war and other public purposes. Contrary to current ideas, lending was not originally developed as a way of financing commerce. The Venetians, Dutch, Henseatic, British and other merchants up to the seventeenth century financed their operations with partners' capital contributions.[2]

Dennis further states,

The Catholic Canonists did not disapprove of profits on commercial ventures, rent for the use of land or the sale of the fruits of the land or other capital. They disapproved of money interest on money lent. During the Reformation Period, interest came to be rationalized mainly by the Protestants in a way to get around Canonist objections. The Catholic Church never abandoned its attitude towards usury, but it acquiesced in, or tolerated loans on, the basis of certain assumptions. This moral acquiescence by the Catholic Church and positive endorsement by the Calvinist traders came to be embodied in laws and thoughts and behavior patterns of modern societies.[3]

The rationalizations Dennis is referring to can be seen in a number of commentaries on the Bible. Even though the Old Testament texts are very clear in their condemnation of interest, this did not keep later scholars

---

[1] Quoted in Qureshi, p. 7.
[2] Quoted in Qureshi, p. 167.
[3] Quoted in Qureshi, p. 167.

from virtually ignoring or seemingly distorting this prohibition.[1] For example, the *Henry's Concise Commentary* to Leviticus 25:37 states:

And thus far this law binds still, but could never be thought binding where money is borrowed for purchase of lands, trade, or other improvements; for there it is reasonable that the lender share with the borrower in the profit. The law here is plainly intended for the relief of the poor, to whom it is sometimes as great a charity to lend freely as to give.

This explanation is refutable on its face as interest has never been about the lender sharing with the borrower in the profit. If that were the case, many of the evils of interest would be removed. Similarly, in the Jameison-Fausset-Brown commentary it states:

"Usury was severely condemned (Psalms 15:5, Ezekiel 18:8,17), but the prohibition cannot be considered as applicable to the modern practice of men in business, borrowing and lending at legal rates of interest."

How did the act go from severely condemned to not possibly being applicable to the "modern practice of men in business"? No logic or proof is offered for such a leap. Similarly, in their commentary on Deuteronomy 23:19-20, the Jameison-Fausset-Brown commentary states:

"Thou shalt not lend upon usury to thy brother . . . Unto a stranger thou mayest lend upon usury--The Israelites lived in a simple state of society, and hence they were encouraged to lend to each other in a friendly way without any hope of gain. But the case was different with foreigners, who, engaged in trade and commerce, borrowed to enlarge their capital, and might reasonably be expected to pay interest on their loans."

Again, no evidence is given for their proposition. (There, however, seems to be attitude that the sacred texts are not able to express themselves properly.) In fact, even a famed economist was willing to provide Biblical commentary: Paul Samuelson wrote in his classic textbook on economics,

---

[1] Many of the followers of such religions expect the Muslims to follow in their footsteps, even though their arguments do not seem reasonable or logical whatsoever. The vast majority of the Muslim scholars throughout the world have, to date, avoided such clear and outright playing and tampering with the texts of the Quran and hadith.

"The Biblical utterances against interest and usury *clearly* refer to loans made for consumption rather than investment purposes."[1]

With the removal of "scholastic" objections, it then became the role of the budding science of economics to justify the paying of interest. This, it turns out, is much more difficult than it sounds. Haberler was certainly correct when he stated,

The theory of interest has for a long time been a weak spot in the science of economics, and the explanation and the determination of the interest rate still gives rise to more disagreement amongst economists than any other branch of general economic theory.[2]

In reality, among economics, "There is not a single adequate and generally accepted theory of interest which can give a sound explanation of the origin and the cause of interest."[3]

---

[1] Paul A. Samuelson, *Economics* (New York: McGraw-Hill Book Company, 1976), p. 605. Emphasis added.
[2] Haberler, *Prosperity and Depression* (1st edition), p. 195. Quoted from Afzal-ur-Rahman, p. 9.
[3] Afzal-ur-Rahman, p. 9.

Interest and Its Role in Economy and Life (٥ of ٨): Explanations and Theories

(English)

الربا وأثره على الحياة والاقتصاد : -٥ نظريات وتفسيرات

(إنجليزي)

Jamaal al-Din Zarabozo

جمال الدين زارابوزو

The mere plethora of opinions attempting to explain the existence of interest and justify its payment—accompanied by the credible critiques of all of these views by noted and respected economists[1] —should be a sign to everyone that something is not quite right. In the history of economic thought, one can find the following theories justifying interest (among others):

(1) The "Colorless" Theories (as Boehm-Bawerk calls them): These were advanced by Adam Smith, Ricardo and other early economists. This theory has many flaws, including confusing interest with gross profit on capital. Ricardo further traced all value of capital back to labor—but somehow he failed to note that it was never labor that was receiving the payment for said value.

(2) The Abstinence Theories: These kinds of theories have popped up every now and then. Economists discovered that "abstinence" may not be a good word to use[2] and would often change it to other terms, such as "waiting" (a la Marshall). Interest is, in essence, the wage one receives for "waiting" or "abstaining" from immediate consumption. This theory failed because it seems to think that savings are solely a function of

---

[1] Virtually any textbook on the history of economic thought provides an analysis of the justifications of interest as well as their critiques. One useful reference is Mark Blaug, *Economic Theory in Retrospect* (Cambridge: Cambridge University Press, 1978). Boehm-Bawerk's classic *Capital and Interest* is a strong indictment against earlier theories of interest, although his own theory is certainly not free of defects. Boehm found the earlier theories to be inconsistent and contradictory and, also, that they failed to give a complete theory of interest, explaining why it is paid and what determines its rate. Also see Qureshi, pp. 11-39; Afzal-ur-Rahman, pp. 9-48.

[2] Senior's abstinence theory "was duly ridiculed by a socialist writer, Lasalle, who remarks, 'The profit of capital is the "wage of abstinence." Happy, even priceless, expression. The ascetic millionaires of Europe like Indian penitents or pillar saints, they stand on one leg each on his column, with straining arm and pendulous body and pallid looks, holding a plate towards the people to collect the wages of their abstinence. In their midst, towering up above all his fellows, as head penitent and ascetic, the Baron Rothschild.'" **Qureshi, p. 17.**

interest, which has been found not to be true.

(3) Productivity Theories: The proponents of this theory see productivity as being inherent in capital and therefore interest is simply the payment for that productivity. The theory, as put forward by Say, assumes that capital produces surplus value but, again, there is no proof to support that claim. The most that one can claim is that some value has been created, which is a payment to capital, but one cannot prove that excess or surplus value has been created, which is the essence of their claim that interest is justified. Of course, these theories also complete ignore the monetary factors when analyzing interest.

(4) Use Theories: "Boehm rejected the validity of the assumption that there was beside each capital good a 'use' thereof which was an independent economic good possessing independent value. He further emphasized that 'in the first place, there simply is no such thing as an independent use of capital,' and, consequently, it can not have independent value, nor by its participation give rise to the 'phenomenon of excess value.' To assume such a use is to create an unwarrantable fiction that contravenes all fact."[1]

(5) Remuneration Theories: This group of economists sees interest as the remuneration of "labor performed" by the capitalist. Although supported by English, French and German economists, perhaps this view needs no comment.

(6) The Eclectic (combination of earlier theories, such as Productivity and Abstinence) Theories: Afzal-ur-Rahman writes:

This line of thought seems to reveal a symptom of dissatisfaction with the doctrine of interest as presented and discussed by the economists of the past and the present. And, as no single theory on the subject is in itself considered satisfactory, people have tried to find a combination of elements from several theories in order to find a satisfactory solution of the problem.[2]

(7) Modern Fructification Theory: Henry George was the developer of this theory but it never carried enough weight to have many, if any, followers.

---

[1] Afzal-ur-Rahman, p. 23.
[2] Afzal-ur-Rahman, p. 30.

(8) Modified Abstinence Theory: Yet another unique theory, proposed by Schellwien; it never had much impact.

(9) The Austrian Theory (The Agio¹ or Time-Preference Theory): This is the view that Boehm-Bawerk himself endorses. According to this theory, interest arises "from a difference in value between present and future goods." Cassel has critiqued this theory in detail. It boils down to being a fancy "waiting" theory.

(10) Monetary Theories (the Loanable Funds Theory, the Liquidity Preference Theory, the Stocks and Flows Theory, the Assets-Preference Approach): More recently, economists have tried to introduce and emphasize the influence of monetary factors into the issue of interest. In reality, though, the emphasis here begins to be switched from why interest is paid to what determines the prevailing rate of interest.

"According to Robertson, interest in liquidity preference theory is reduced to nothing more than a risk-premium against fluctuations about which we are not certain. It leaves interest suspended, so to speak in a void, there being interest because there is interest."[2] Similar critiques have been made of the other views in this family of theories.

(11) Exploitation theory: Incidentally, socialist economists have always considered interest as nothing but exploitation. It should be recalled that the "founding fathers" of capitalist theory, Adam Smith and Ricardo, believed that the source of all value is nothing but labor. If that is true, then all payments should be made to labor and interest is nothing but exploitation.

In a couple of places, Afzal-ur-Rahman has provided excellent conclusions concerning these different theories of interest. He stated:

A critical study of the historical development of the phenomenon of interest has shown that interest is paid to an independent factor of production, which may be called either waiting or postponement or abstinence or use etc. But all these theories have failed to answer or to prove as to why interest is paid or should be paid to this factor.

---

[1] "Agio" is the premium which one is willing to pay for the present goods as compared to having the same goods in future.
[2] Afzal-ur-Rahman, p. 44.

Some point to the necessity of waiting; others to the necessity of abstinence of postponement; but none of these explanations answer the question.

Neither mere necessity of waiting or postponement or abstinence nor mere use or productivity of capital is enough to prove that interest is a necessary payment for the employment of capital in production. Besides, these theories have failed to answer how a variable factor can possibly determine a fixed factor like the rate of interest? How could such a theory be valid or tenable?[1]

Later he writes:

The monetary theories, like marginal productivity theories, have made no attempt to answer the question: why should interest be paid? Or why interest is paid? They have simply ignored this question and have sought refuge in the theory of value.

They say, like all other things, the price of capital is determined by the demand for and supply of money. But it seems that they have forgotten the basic difference between the two problems; the theory of value is a problem of exchange, while theory of interest is a problem of distribution.

Both loanable funds and liquidity preference theories are basically supply and demand theories of interest and explain it with reference to supply of and demand for loanable funds and money respectively.

But they do not give any justification for the phenomenon of interest. Even if capital has a right to proper compensation as a reward for its contribution to the creation of wealth, "it can only draw its share from the increase of national wealth only to the extent of its contribution to it. It cannot be allowed to run away with its pound of flesh, determined in advance, and unrelated to the actualities of production."[2]

According to Boehm Bawerk, the study of all these theories "reveals the development of three essentially divergent basic conceptions of the interest problem." One group, the representatives of the productivity theory, treats the interest problem as a problem of production.

---

[1] Afzal-ur-Rahman, pp. 37-38.
[2] Afzal-ur-Rahman quoted this Ahmad, *The Economics of Islam*.

The socialist-exponents of the exploitation theories treat the interest problem as purely a problem of distribution; while the third group, the supporters of the monetary theories, seeks in the theory of interest, the problem of value.

There is no doubt that all these theorists, having been confused by the very magnanimity and pervasiveness of the phenomenon of interest, have avoided the main issue as to why interest should be paid? They have, indeed, spent all their energies in solving the problem either of waiting or abstinence or productivity or "labor value" or "the determination of value" and have not said anything about the origin or the justification of the institution of interest.[1]

---

[1] Afzal-ur-Rahman, pp. 46-47.

Interest and Its Role in Economy and Life (6 of 8):
Ills of Interest (1)

(English)

الربا وأثره على الحياة والاقتصاد : ٦- عواقب الربا (أ)

(إنجليزي)

Jamaal al-Din Zarabozo

جمال الدين زارابوزو

The Ills of Interest

Economists can attempt to come up with numerous justifications for the payment of interest but the real test is to study the affects that interest has. It is important to note that when something is prohibited by God, this does not mean that there is absolutely nothing beneficial in the prohibited item or practice. Indeed, one may be able to find something beneficial even in prohibited items. For example, God says in the Quran about alcohol:

"They ask you [O Muhammad] concerning wine and gambling. Say: 'In them is great sin, and some benefit for people; but the sin of them is greater than the benefit...'" (Quran 2:219)

Thus, the essential point is not whether there is anything beneficial in something but whether the harm of something outweighs its benefit. Thus, economists may be able to find a hint of a justification for paying interest but this definitely would not outweigh the harms that interest can be shown to cause, as shall be discussed in this section.

Even if interest is considered some kind of payment to a factor of production, it has some unique characteristics that set it apart from payments to any other factor of production. Due to its unique nature, it leads to some very disturbing results.

First, interest leads to an inequitable distribution of income. This can be seen by taking an example of three people. Suppose there are three people who consume of all of their income in a given year yet one of them starts with $1,000 in savings, a second with $100 and a third with zero. At 10% interest per annum, by the end of the year, the first person will have $1,100, the second $110 and the third person zero in their accounts. If the same scenario follows in the next year, the first person will have $1,210, the second $121 and the third will have zero.

Already, one can see how the distribution between them grows every year, even between the one who has some savings of his own. This scenario will be made even worse if the richest person will also to be able to add savings. Suppose he adds one thousand at the end of each year. He will have 1,100 at the end of the first year, he adds $1,000 and continues with his 10% interest and he will have $2,310 at the end of the second year, and so on.

Now it is one thing if this money paid was actually due to some positive factor of production but in reality one cannot make that argument in this case. The money that the people are making via interest may have been squandered, lost or even stolen by the people who borrowed it, but one still has to be pay the interest. It may have been invested in a completely losing project and therefore it actually did not produce anything.

But all of that does not matter, it has to be paid regardless of whether that "factor of production" produces anything or not. This is simply one of the unique aspects of money and payments to money. No one can argue that this is just and therefore its results are an inequitable distribution of money.

Furthermore, the distribution of income becomes more and more skewed over time. One can imagine some individuals dealing in millions while others are dealing in hundreds or thousands. The disparity in their interest incomes will indeed be great and growing every year. In other words, as one hears often, it will lead to a situation where the rich keep getting richer while the poor keep getting relatively poorer.

Note that those in debt, paying interest that grows every year, have not been added to the equation. In their case, as interest continues to grow, more and more of their overall income is consumed by interest, further exacerbating the skewed distribution of income.

Someone could ask as to whether an inequitable distribution of income should be considered a major issue. Besides the psychological effects on the poor, especially given mass media advertising that emphasizes the good life and the need to consume, there are very important effects on the market as a whole.

In a market economy, production will be geared towards those who have the money to pay for the output, regardless of how necessary other goods may be for society. If the rich desire, demand and are willing to pay a lot of money for SUVs and gas-guzzling vehicles, those will be produced (regardless of how much conservationists may complain). As the income distribution becomes more and more skewed, more and more resources will be devoted to the demands of the richer classes.

Since resources are somewhat "fixed," this means that less and less will be devoted to the needs of the poorer classes. Furthermore, the lesser resources devoted to the goods that the poor consume reduces supply and drives up the prices of those goods, further harming the poor people's overall economic situation. For example, one can find numerous medical clinics catering to the rich (those who can afford such treatments), even if they are far from necessary, such as numerous places for cosmetic surgery and the like.

At the same time, one may find it very difficult to find clinics catering to the poor and meeting their basic needs. If they could pay more for those essential services, in a market driven economy, one would definitely find more of those types of clinics, more resources devoted to those needs and a cheaper price in the long-run for what they need. (In addition, this skewed distribution also has strong implications for the health of democracy; however, that discussion is beyond the scope of this paper.)

In addition, the burden of interest upon the poor who fall into debt puts them into a situation where they cannot advance socially or economically, widening the gap between the rich and the poor. Debt itself is a difficult situation for any individual. However, it is interest payments that make one's debt a moving target, many times one that an individual simply cannot keep up with. Again, it is a bogus factor of production but it works to allow the rich to get richer while putting a great burden upon those who fall into debt.

Perhaps all the readers are familiar with how much of a debtor society the United States, the richest country in the world, has become. This has afflicted not only the lower classes but many of the middle class as well. Some sorry individuals do not realize that if they pay only the minimum on their credit card bills, for example, they will virtually never clear their balance.[1]

But, of course, it is the poorest that are hardest hit. In fact, the system is stacked against them as the poorer an individual is, the worst his credit rating and the higher the interest rate he will be forced to pay. Mirza Shahjahan's *Income, Debt and the Quest for Rich America The Economic Tale*

---

[1] Shahjahan notes, "Most households are not really aware of the degree of erosion of their income which results from high interest payments on outstanding debts." Mirza Shahjahan, *Income, Debt and the Quest for Rich America: The Economic Tale of Small and Mid-Sized US Cities* (Beltsville, MD: Writers' Inc. International, 2000), p. 103.

of Small and Mid-Sized US Cities is a study of how debt and its corresponding interest burden has afflicted much of "middle America."[1]

The plight of small-scale farmers forced to borrow due to dropping prices on their output has been well-documented. Many of them have pawned their precious belongings or lost their farms that have been in their families for generations simply due to interest payments that they could not keep up with. Shahjahan found that some of the poor pay over 15% of their yearly income on interest payments alone (with most paying between 8% and 12%)—not to mention the burden of calls and threats from creditors that the poor often receive. In Shahjahan's conclusions, he states:

Both the monetary and real burdens of debt have kept many debtors in a lifelong struggle to service their debts. The average size of the debt of indebted households for the 1990-1993 period was $32,493, equaling almost 100% of these households' income. Our estimate of per capita household debt for 1990-1993 amounts to $12,571. Debt of this magnitude, combined with a temporary job and low income, can be depressing and produce overwhelming psychological conditions...

Some households' interest payments exceed 15% of their income. This high interest cost has been a source of significant erosion of household income...

Most households – millions in number – in mid-sized cities struggle day in and day out to meet their basic needs of life. Thousands of them fail to provide a decent life for their families or support the higher education of their children. They live in debt and die in debt. This situation makes them feel that they live less than a full life...

These households are caught in a situation of economic servitude where the most obvious escape routes are blocked by institutional forces. Acquiring skills or higher education could be the key that opens the way to real opportunity, but higher education is expensive and beyond the reach of most of the households in these cities. These households have no opportunity to excel and find themselves passed over for the positions they had hoped for. This is the nature of the plight of the working class families in the small and mid-sized cities of our nation.[2]

---

[1] Shahjahan, *passim*.
[2] Shahjahan, pp. 224-236.

Interest and Its Role in Economy and Life (7 of 8):
Ills of Interest (2)

(English)

الربا وأثره على الحياة والاقتصاد : ٧- عواقب الربا (ب)

(إنجليزي)

Jamaal al-Din Zarabozo

جمال الدين زارابوزو

On an international level, the situation is much more devastating and dangerous. There is no question that when looked at from an international perspective, interest kills people. The debt servicing of lesser developed countries today is so great that they must sacrifice essential health and nutritional needs.

It is dumbfounding to think that untold numbers of children are dying daily in lesser-developed countries due to the "tool" of modern capitalism: interest. Some African governments are forced to spend more on debt servicing than they spend on health or education.[1]

In this context, the UNDP (1998) predicted that if the external debt of the 20 poorest countries of the world was written off, it could save the lives of 20 million people before the year 2000. In other words, it means that uncancelled debt was responsible for the deaths of 130,000 children a week up until the year 2000.[2]

Ken Livingston, Mayor of London, claimed that global capitalism kills more people each year then were killed by Adolf Hitler. He blamed the IMF and World Bank for deaths of millions due to their refusal to ease the debt burden.

Susan George stated that every year since 1981 between 15 and 20 million people died unnecessarily due to debt burden "because Third World governments have had to cut back on clean water and health programs to meet their repayments."[3]

Debt, with its increasing amount of interest compounded upon it, is dangerous for any nation because it means loss of sovereignty and control.[4]

---

[1] Cf., Noreena Hertz. *The Debt Threat* (New York: HarperBusiness, 2004), p. 3.
[2] Ali Mohammadi and Muhammad Ahsan, *Globalisation or Reconolisation? The Muslim World in the 21st Century* (London: Ta-Ha Publishers, Ltd. 2002), p. 38.
[3] Mohammadi and Muhammad Ahsan, p. 43.
[4] Again, simply the removal of interest from such debts would work wonders to alleviate the position of the world's poorest. The amount of interest paid by these poor countries is astronomical. **Caufield noted,** "By 1978, one-quarter of all the money borrowed by non-OPEC Third World countries was used to pay interest on existing debt. The situation was particularly bad in Latin America, where borrowing doubled between 1976 and 1982, and 70 percent of new loans went to pay interest on old debt... By 1982, the situation had become truly absurd. Latin America was owing hundreds of billions of dollars a year, and spending all of it— more—on keeping up payments on its past debts." **Catherine Caufield,** *Masters of Illusion: The World Bank and the Poverty of Nations* (London, England: Pan Books, 1996), p.

This aspect, incidentally, is no accident. Lesser developed countries—especially their elites and corrupt rulers—are not free of guilt when it comes to the issue of the debt that they have accumulated. At the same time, if they did not borrow and get in debt, pressure would definitely be put on them to do so. Caufield noted:

Thus it has been with the World Bank; refunding operations have become more and more of the total of its lending. The result has been an accumulation of debt by the Bank's borrowers—and a gradual loss of sovereignty as well. No creditor is willing to keep refunding forever without asserting some control over the way the debtor conducts business. In earlier times, the great powers did not hesitate to use military force to bend recalcitrant debtors to their will. In his classic essay, "Public Debts," published in 1887, the American economist Henry Carter Adams wrote that "the granting of foreign credits is the first step toward the establishment of an aggressive foreign policy, and under certain condition, leads inevitably to conquest and occupation"

The Bank's approach to its debtors is not so crude. Instead of sending in the Marines, it offers advice on how countries should manage their finances, make their laws, provide services to their people, and conduct themselves in the international market. Its powers of persuasion are great, due to the universal conviction that, should it decide to ostracize a borrower, all other major national and international powers will follow its lead. Thus, by the excessive lending—born of an underlying inconsistency its mission—the Bank has added to its own power and depleted that of its borrowers.[1]

---

137. Even when "debt relief" is granted, payments are delayed but it is demanded that the interest still accumulates on it. According to Gwynne, "Even though the banks may allow a country such as Poland to 'reschedule' its debt—allowing it twenty years instead of ten to repay, for example—the interest payments keep coming. And it is interest that shores up the bottom line of a bank's profit-and-loss statement." S. C. Gwynne, "Selling Money-and Dependency: Setting the Debt Trap," in Steven Hiatt, ed. *A Game as Old as Empire: The Secret World of Economic Hit Men and the Web of Global Corruption* (San Francisco: Berrett-Koehler Publishers, Inc., 2007), p. 35. Payer noted this phenomenon all the way back in 1974, but virtually nothing has been done to correct it. See Cheryl Payer, *The Debt Trap: The International Monetary Fund and the Third World* (New York: Monthly Review Press, 1974), p 46.

[1] Caufield, p. 336

John Perkins' now famous *Confessions of an Economic Hit Man* [1] details contemporary economic intrigues. While describing his job of evaluating projects, he wrote:

The unspoken aspect of every one of these projects was that they were intended to create large profits for the contractors, and to make a handful of wealthy and influential families in the receiving countries very happy, while assuring the long-term financial dependence and therefore the political loyalty of governments around the world. The larger the loan, the better. The fact that the debt burden placed on a country would deprive its poorest citizens of health, education, and other social services for decades to come was not taken into consideration. [2]

Perkins' work has now been followed up by *A Game as Old as Empire: The Secret World of Economic Hit Men* and the *Web of Global Corruption* edited by Steven Hiatt. [3] Hiatt writes,

Debt keeps Third World countries under control. Dependent on aid, loan reschedulings, and debt rollovers to survive—never mind actually develop— they have been forced to restructure their economies and rewrite their laws to meet conditions laid down in IMF structural adjustment programs and World Bank conditionalities. [4]

The current debt situation, with the major role that interest is playing in it, is potentially very devastating for the world as a whole. In *Global Trends 2015*, the Central Intelligence Agency (CIA) recognized:

The rising tide of the global economy will create many economic winners, but it will not lift all boats. [It will] spawn conflicts at home and abroad ensuring an ever-wider gap between regional winners and losers than exists today. [Globalization's] evolution will be rocky, marked by chronic financial volatility and a widening economic divide. Regions, countries and groups feeling left behind will face deepening economic stagnation, political instability and cultural alienation. They will foster political, eth-

---

[1] John Perkins, *Confessions of an Economic Hit Man* (San Francisco: Berrett-Koehler Publishers Inc., 2004), *passim*.
[2] Perkins, p. 15.
[3] Steven Hiatt, ed. *A Game as Old as Empire: The Secret World of Economic Hit Men and the Web of Global Corruption* (San Francisco: Berrett-Koehler Publishers, Inc., 2007)
[4] Hiatt, p. 23.

nic, ideological and religious extremism, along with the violence that often accompanies it.[1]

Noreena Hertz has an excellent chapter in her work, *The Debt Threat: How debt is destroying the developing world... and threatening us all*, delineating many of the dangers that the massive debt—and, again, which would not be as massive without the ever-growing aspect of interest—poses for the world today. She details the dangers of extremism, terrorism, depletion of the world's natural resources, and more. To cite just one aspect, she writes:

Debt's ugly progeny—poverty, inequality, and injustice—are also called upon to justify, and even legitimize, acts of the greatest violence. Only a few weeks after the World Trade Center was attacked, leading African commentator Michael Fortin wrote: "We have to recognize that this deplorable act of aggression may have been, at least in part, an act of revenge on the part of desperate and humiliated people, crushed by the weight of the economic oppression practiced by the peoples of the West." Fortin's language—"crushed," "oppression," "desperate," "humiliated"—is deliberately evocative. And it is manifestly clear that there is an audience with whom such words powerfully resonate.[2]

In reality, there are yet other ills related to interest that could be discussed but the above should suffice for the purposes here.

---

[1] Quoted from Hertz, p. 156.
[2] Hertz, p. 161.

Interest and Its Role in Economy and Life (8 of 8): The Islamic Solution

(English)

الربا وأثره على الحياة والاقتصاد : ٨- الحل الإسلامي

(إنجليزي)

Jamaal al-Din Zarabozo

جمال الدين زارابوزو

The Islamic Solution

The Islamic solution to the issue of interest rests upon two basic principles:

(1) If an individual wishes to lend money to another in order to help the latter, this act must be based on "brotherly principles" and it is absolutely unacceptable to charge any interest in such a case. It is not helping another individual to put him into a cycle of debt where he has to pay more than what they borrowed. This principle applies as well to Islamic international relations. If this important principle were applied today, countries would truly give "aid" and assistance to other countries, rather than sucking them into a pattern of dependency and debt burden.

(2) If an individual wishes to use his money to make more money, then he must be willing to put his money at risk. In other words, he cannot guarantee for himself a fixed return (whose amount keeps growing over time) regardless of the result of the investment that his money is used for. If he puts his money at risk, he is deserving of some share of the profits. However, this also means that he must accept losses if losses occur. This is a system that is based on justice. It also has numerous benefits to it. The one who invests becomes concerned about the results of his investment and cannot demand his "pound of flesh" regardless of what may occur to the debtor.

This Islamic solution works for individuals as well as for society as a whole. Banks are essentially financial intermediaries. They take money from those who have excess money (savings) and turn it over to those who need money for investment purposes.

Interest is not necessary for such a system to work. The bank and its depositors (shareholders) invest, rather than simply loan, their holdings.

The money is put at risk and the return to the depositors will be based on the amount of profits made in the respective investments. Under normal circumstances of a growing economy, if the bank is big enough and it diversifies its portfolio, the bank is virtually "guaranteed" a positive return on its total investments. Thus, those who invest their money with the bank will also receive a positive return on their money without it being guaranteed or fixed ahead of time.

Numerous "Islamic" financial institutions have been set up throughout the world today. They have been established on the principle of avoiding interest and some of them have flourished.[1]

Conclusions

For the most part, "modern civilization" has decided to turn its back on Divine Guidance (mostly due to the experience in the West with Christianity) and have attempted to construct their own economic systems, political systems, international laws and so on. When doing so, though, they have to admit that they are attempting something that is beyond their means. The social sciences are very different from the physical sciences. There are no labs in which humans can be entered to determine what may be the best results under different scenarios (and even that would have to assume that humans will always react the same under the same circumstances).

In the realm of economics, the first thing that may come to mind is the collapse of the theories of socialism and communism. One should, though, also take a closer look at capitalism and how far its reality is from what it is supposed to be. The early capitalist theorists envisioned a theory that would lead to "the best of all possible worlds." However, their theories were based on assumptions that never were and will never be fulfilled. They assumed perfect competition, perfect knowledge, free trade and so forth. Once these assumptions are violated, which they inevitably are, they do not lead to the "best of all possible worlds."Instead, they easily lead to a world of exploitation, wherein the rich get richer and the poor get poorer. One of the diving forces behind this system is the institutionalization of interest.

God has blessed humans with the guidance of the Quran—a book that has been minutely preserved since its revelation. This book contains the guidance that humankind needs to lead a successful life in both this world and the Hereafter. It is therefore no surprise that this book absolutely prohibits and condemns interest in the strongest fashion.

---

[1] For more details on the theoretical and practical workings of such institutions, see El-Gousi, pp. 199-247; Frank E. Vogel and Samuel L. Hayes III, *Islamic Law and Finance: Religion, Risk, and Return* (The Hague: Kluwer Law International, 1998), pp. 181-295.

www.ingramcontent.com/pod-product-compliance
Lightning Source LLC
Chambersburg PA
CBHW071127030426
42336CB00013BA/2230